The ABC's of Spiritual Identity

By Lottie Alexander

The ABC's of Spiritual Identity

Copyright © 2025

All rights reserved. No part of this publication may be reproduced, stored in a retrieval system, or transmitted in any form by any means, for example, electronic, photocopy, recording, scanning, or other without prior written permission of the publisher. The only exception is brief quotations in printed reviews.

Dedication

I dedicate this book to my mother, Mary Russaw. Today, she is suffering from a disease called vascular dementia. This is a state of mind that has limited her ability to be mentally present in the world as we know it. She struggles daily to process information, to articulate her thoughts and to express her true feelings. She has lost contact with who she truly is, in a real sense.

But then there is another layer of identity that is so very important to humanity's existence. Yes, every person on this earth is known by Our Creator! God decided who we should be, even before we were born! But, how many of you are there, who right at this very moment, have not discovered who God says you are? I have good news for you! You can get started on your journey of discovery right now!

So, I dedicate "The A, B, C's of Spiritual Identity" to every man, woman, boy and girl who is struggling in this area. No, I do not know you; but, God does! God knows each of us by name and He pre-ordained each of us for our own unique purpose. According to Jeremiah 1, verse five, God knew you before you were conceived in your mother's womb. Your name is written on the table of God's heart, and your face is etched in the palm of His Hand. God created you and me on purpose...for purpose.

You are "fearfully and wonderfully made"! God took his time to intricately design you. According to Scripture, He spoke everything else into existence. But He fashioned you and me with his own hand. It is so important that you know who God says you are because then no one else can define you. Jesus did not ask his disciples, "Who do men say that I am?" because he did not already know the answer. In the final analysis, it didn't matter. He went on to carry out the will of his Father, despite what others thought or said about him.

You are an unrepeatable, historical event! There is only one you! You cannot be duplicated or copied. You are the only version of you that there will ever be! You are uniquely special. God loves you just the way you are. Yet, He wants more for you than you can even imagine.

"The A, B, C's of Spiritual Identity" is a divinely inspired book that I believe will encourage you to become who God created and called you to be. You are called to "greatness"! Go, be great!

-Lottie

The ABC's of Spiritual Identity

Book Contents

Introduction......................Page 9

Accepted.........................Page 19

Blessed...........................Page 20

Chosen............................Page 22

Delivered........................Page 24

Empowered.....................Page 26

Fearfully & Wonderfully Made...............................Page 28

Gifted..............................Page 30

His..................................Page 32

[God's] Image..................Page 34

Justified..........................Page 36

Kingdom Citizen.............Page 38

Loved ....Page 40

More Than
a Conqueror....................Page 42

New Creature..................Page 44

Overcomer.......................Page 46

Processed For Purpose......Page 48

Quickened........................Page 50

Redeemed........................Page 52

Sanctified........................Page 54

Triumphant.....................Page 56

"Un"................................Page 58

Valuable..........................Page 60

Who God Says I Am.........Page 62

Xerophyte..........................*Page 64*

Yokefellow of
Jesus Christ........................*Page 66*

Zionist................................*Page 68*

Introduction

From very early on in life, a baby's identity begins to be formulated. Although a child is given an actual birth name, he/she responds to whatever name others call them most of the time. Imagine if what a child is called is actually not a name but a descriptor such as ugly, worthless, dumb, etc. A child may be too young to know or understand what those descriptors mean; but, the spirit behind them embeds itself in that child's psyche. When that child grows up, how he/she has been identified will likely determine what they believe concerning who they are. Consequently, the behaviors attached to those identifiers will eventually begin to emerge. In the same manner, a child who grows up in a sound, stable and nurturing environment, who is appropriately identified, will likely have a healthier sense of their identity.

Paul wrote to the Corinthian church, "Any man in Christ is a new creature. Old things are passed away and behold all things are become new." 2 Corinthians 5:17 (KJV). Throughout Scripture, God demonstrated how vital a name is. Key figures, both men *and women of the Bible, started out with one name. But as the purpose of God was revealed in their lives, God changed their names.*

This is a strong indication of how significant identity is. I believe that spiritual identity is even more important. It is my belief that how one views him/herself has a strong impact on how they view others. So, it is critical that we tap into our God-given spiritual identity. Our sense of identity shapes our perspective concerning our own self-worth. Those with whom we interact do not have to regard us in the same way as we view ourselves. Many people may inaccurately define others and put labels on them. But one who has a strong sense of who he/she is, will likely not allow others to define who they are.

As it relates to this subject matter, it suffices to say that, on some level, all of us have been challenged in the area of spiritual identity. Because of how God has dealt with me concerning this topic, I now believe that "spiritual identity" cannot, and should not, be ignored. It is one of the building blocks on which Kingdom ministry rests! "The A-B-C's of Spiritual Identity" is a 26-

week journey that was birthed out of my own desire to overcome the spirit of rejection. As I began this journey, I found that this spirit was able to operate in my life because I did not fully understand who I was in God. Through the Scripture passages that God gave me, He unlocked my prison door and freed me from the bondage that had held me captive for the better part of my life. I am still learning how to walk in my liberty; but, I am not the same person that I was before!

Luke 22:32 declares, "And when thou art converted, strengthen thy brethren." Therefore, this is why I now believe I must share the Scriptures with you that helped me in this area. It is my Christian obligation. Even if you are now a victor over this stronghold, you may know someone who will benefit from the information in this book. Get ready to leave where you are to move to higher ground!! Do not look back but stay focused on God and follow His leading!! It's time!! Let's go!!!

The ABC's of Spiritual Identity

I AM ACCEPTED IN THE BELOVED

I AM BLESSED

I AM CHOSEN

I AM DELIVERED

I AM EMPOWERED

I AM FEARFULLY AND WONDERFULLY MADE

I AM FORGIVEN

I AM A FRIEND OF GOD

The ABC's of Spiritual Identity

I AM GIFTED

I AM HIS

I HAVE A NEW IDENTITY

I AM JUSTIFIED

I AM A KINGDOM CITIZEN

I AM LED BY GOD

I AM MORE THAN A CONQUEROR

The ABC's of Spiritual Identity

I AM A NEW CREATURE

I AM AN OVERCOMER

I HAVE BEEN PROCESSED FOR PURPOSE

I AM QUICKENED

I AM REDEEMED

I AM SANCTIFIED

I AM TRIUMPHANT

The ABC's of Spiritual Identity

I AM THE "UN"

I AM VALUABLE

I AM WHO GOD SAYS I AM

I AM A XEROPHYTE

I AM A YOKE FELLOW OF JESUS CHRIST

I AM A ZIONIST

The ABC's of Spiritual Identity

Accepted

To receive with favor; to approve of; to acknowledge; to include.

Ephesians 1:6 To the praise of the glory of His grace, wherein he hath made us accepted in the beloved.

PRAYER: May every believer be encouraged to always remember that you matter to God! In Jesus Name...Amen

B

Blessed

Happiness that does not exist because of favorable conditions; a spiritual state of satisfaction, fulfillment, and contentment that is birthed out of one's relationship with God.

<u>Ephesians 1:3</u> *Blessed be the God and Father of our Lord Jesus Christ, who hath blessed us with all spiritual blessings in heavenly places in Christ.*

The ABC's of Spiritual Identity

PRAYER: *Lord, may I forever be reminded that no matter what happens in my life, I am still blessed because it is all working for my good! Amen!!*

C

Chosen

Selected as a result of an intentional decision; preferred; carefully hand-picked.

Ephesians 1:4 According as he hath chosen us in Him before the foundation of the world, that we should be holy and without blame before him in love.

PRAYER: Heavenly Father, thank you that I have been chosen to be a member of your family. I walk in

Sonship with you, having been adopted into the family of God through the blood of Jesus Christ, your beloved Son! Amen!!

D

Delivered

Set free; freed from penalty; rescued from harm; saved from evil or trouble; liberated; emancipated; released from slavery; no longer bound or in bondage.

<u>Colossians 1:12a, 13</u> Giving thanks unto the Father...Who hath delivered us from the power of darkness, and hath translated us into the kingdom of his dear Son.

PRAYER: *Sovereign God, how gracious and merciful You are! You have delivered me from the penalty of sin, which is death. Because of Your mercy, I have now been given new life!! Amen!! Thank You Lord!!*

E

Empowered

To give authority to; to enable; to permit; to authorize, commission or license.

Acts 1:8 But ye shall receive power; after that the Holy Ghost is come upon you: and ye shall be witnesses unto me both in Jerusalem, and in all Judaea, and in Samaria, and unto the uttermost part of the earth.

PRAYER: *Thank You Omnipotent God for empowering me to accomplish great things, to witness to others and to live holy. Through the power of Your Holy Spirit, I can do what I cannot do in my own strength. Glory to Your Name, Lord God Almighty!! Amen!!*

The ABC's of Spiritual Identity

Fearfully & Wonderfully Made

Carefully and intricately designed; Crafted with precision and much attention to detail; Intentionally created to be rare and unique; Unable to be duplicated; Authentically fashioned.

Psalms 138:14a *I will praise thee; for I am fearfully and wonderfully made...*

The ABC's of Spiritual Identity

<u>*PRAYER*</u>*: There will never be another "me"! Thank You, Heavenly Father for reminding me not to be overly concerned about what others think about me. I am grateful, Lord God, that I no longer have to question whether or not I am "good enough." I finally understand that though I am not perfect, I am the best version of "me" there will ever be!! Amen!!*

G

Gifted

Possessing a natural ability or special talent; that which is received not as the result of personal merit or effort; symbolizing or representing that which is accepted, not earned.

Ephesians 4:8, 11-13 Wherefore he saith, When he ascended up on high, he led captivity captive, and gave gifts unto men. And he gave some, apostles; and some, prophets; and some, evangelists; and some, pastors and teachers; For the perfecting of the saints, for the work of the ministry, for the edifying of the body of Christ.

PRAYER: Lord God, wherever my place in the Body is, help me to effectively function in that capacity. I acknowledge that this is part of my purpose that I must fulfill in the earth until Jesus comes. Amen!!

The ABC's of Spiritual Identity

H

His

Belonging to [God]; made in His likeness and image; created to mirror and reflect Who God Is...His character, His attributes and His ways.

1 Corinthians 6:19, 20a What? Know ye not that ye...are not your own? For ye are bought with a price...

PRAYER: Lover of my soul, I can never repay the debt I owe You! So, remind me daily that my reasonable *service is to present myself...my body and my entire being...a living sacrifice, holy and acceptable unto You, Father God.*

The ABC's of Spiritual Identity

I

[God's] **Image**

A reflection of someone or something; A mirrored projection of a living being or tangible object (the image itself is not real; but, looks exactly like the person or thing it is a reflection of).

<u>Genesis 1:27</u> So God created man in his own image, in the image of God created he him; male and female created he them.

PRAYER: God, You created humanity to look just like you!!! What an awesome God You Are! How marvelous are the works of Your Hands. May I resemble you more each day. I pray that my life will model the example of YOUR dear son, Jesus Christ...humanity's perfect example! Thank YOU, Oh holy God!! Amen!!

J

Justified

Cleared of all blame or guilt; In a legal sense…to show a satisfactory reason or excuse for one's actions. In the case of why humanity sinned against God, there was no justification. God's justification for pardoning us was simply because He loves us!!

St. John 3:16 *For God so loved the world, that he gave his only begotten Son, that whosoever believeth in him should not perish, but have everlasting life.*

PRAYER: *Merciful and gracious God! Truly we owe you a debt that we will never be able to repay you! Thank You for the gift of eternal life…provided unto us because of your great love for us. Our sin debt was paid for with the blood of Your dear Son, Jesus Christ!! Oh, what a loving God You Are! Amen!!*

The ABC's of Spiritual Identity

[A] Kingdom Citizen

Kingdom is a country, realm, domain, province or place where the governing authority is a king or queen. A Kingdom Citizen is one who resides in such a place. God's people are citizens of the Kingdom of God!

Romans 14:17, 18 The Kingdom of God is not meat and drink; but righteousness, and peace, and joy in the Holy Ghost. For he that in these things serveth Christ is acceptable to God, and approved of men.

PRAYER: Thank You Father, for the privilege to become citizens of Your Kingdom! You could have cast us away; but, instead, you have drawn us in. You welcomed us to occupy this place in You even though we deserved to be discarded. The blood of Your Son, Jesus, reserved our seat in Your Kingdom! Halleluiah!!

L

Loved

A strong liking; a warm, fond or tender feeling; the kindly feeling of God for his creatures or the reverent devotion due from them to God.

In all this, the God-kind of love is that which is more than just a feeling. God's unconditional love transcends feelings and continues to operate, even when human love runs out.

Romans 5:8 *But God commended his love toward us, in that, while we were yet sinners, <u>Christ died for us.</u>*

PRAYER: *God, we will never be able to understand the depth of this great love you have bestowed upon us! We lift our hands in total adoration unto You! We give You praise, honor and glory because that is what You are due! We pray that as recipients of Your love, we will freely share that same love with those whom we live and interact with daily! In Jesus Name...Amen!!*

M

More Than a Conqueror

A conqueror is one who actually engages in combat and defeats his/her opponent. One who is more than a conqueror shows up for the contest; but, because the battle is already fixed, he is deemed a conqueror even though he/she does not have to physically engage in the fight.

1 Samuel 17:47 And all this assembly shall know that the LORD saveth not with sword and spear: for the battle is the LORD's, and he will give you into our hands.

PRAYER: Jehovah Sabaoth, how grateful we are that we can trust You to be there with and for us in the midst of every challenge we face. You are Omnipotent, Omniscient and Omnipresent!! You are Mighty in battle!! We are engaged in a fight with an enemy that we cannot see; but, Your eyes behold everything...even our invisible foe! Thank you for fighting for us and for securing our certain victory in You! Amen!!

[A] New Creature

Not the same; different; never having existed before; changed; fresh; unused; unfamiliar; strange.

<u>2 Corinthians 5:17</u> *Therefore if any man be in Christ, he is a new creature: old things are passed away; behold, all things are become new.*

<u>**PRAYER**</u>: *Miracle working God, every time I look back over my life and I remember from whence I have come, I*

The ABC's of Spiritual Identity

cannot help but to praise you!! I stand in awe of how You took the ugliness of my past and made something beautiful out of my life!! I don't look like what I have been through! You don't label me by what I've done! I now walk in the beauty of holiness and in the newness of life! You call me Your child and You removed the stench of sin off of me! I offer You my praise as a sweet-smelling savor in Your nostrils! Glory!!! Amen!!

O

[An] Overcomer

One who faces afflictions, obstacles and adversity with a victory mindset; one who does not give in to the temptation to quit or to give up when he/she encounters challenging situations. The adverse situation may not change over a short period of time. But, the overcomer, because of his "winning" mindset, comes out of the test changed for the better!

<u>St. John 16:33</u> These things have I spoken unto you that in me ye might

have peace. In the world ye shall have tribulation: but be of good cheer; I have overcome the world.

<u>1 John 4:4</u> Ye are of God, little children, and have overcome them: because greater is he that is in you, than he that is in the world.

<u>PRAYER:</u> Thank you, my God, that I don't have to be anxious about the things that concern me in this life. When life seems unbearable, I can cast my cares on you. I am an overcomer because You are my God who carries my burdens and fights my battles for me! Amen!!

P

[Being] **Processed For Purpose**

Process – How God shapes me into who and what He pre-destined me to be.

Purpose – What God intends to accomplish through my life here on earth!

Romans 8:28. And we know that all things work together for good to them that love God, to them who are the called according to his purpose.

PRAYER: *God, I have come to understand that even the things that I perceive as bad, You will turn them for my good. No part of my life is wasted! You are still the same God, who spoke this world into existence and created humanity from dust! Your "revealed" purpose is what makes my life make sense. Glory to You, my God...Almighty Creator!*

Q

Quickened

Made alive; brought back to life; resurrected;

Ephesians 2:1, 5 And you hath he quickened, who were dead in trespasses and sins; Even when we were dead in sins, hath quickened us together with Christ, (by grace ye are saved;)

PRAYER: I realize that it is not because of any good of my own that I have been given another chance at life!

I was a wretched sinner. My plight was death; yet, You gave me the gift of "new" life through Your Son...my Saviour, Jesus Christ. Surely, my soul was doomed to live eternally in hell had it not been for your love for me. Thank You Heavenly Father!!

R

Redeemed

Paid a price in order to secure the release of something or someone; paid the required ransom to liberate one from oppression, enslavement or another type of binding obligation.

Ephesians 3: 13 Christ hath redeemed us from the curse of the law, being made a curse for us: for it is written, Cursed is every one that hangeth on a tree.

PRAYER: Jesus, your death satisfied the penalty for my sin, which was according to the law!! I owed a debt that I could not pay! Thank You Jesus, for paying the debt for sin, that you did not owe! You gave your life in exchange for mine! You are my strength and my Redeemer!! Amen!!

S

Sanctified

Set apart as sacred [belonging to or dedicated to God]; consecrated [observed as holy] to carry out special service unto God; reserved for a sacrificial offering unto God.

<u>Jeremiah 1:5</u> Before I formed thee in the belly I knew thee; and before thou camest forth out of the womb I sanctified thee, and I ordained thee a prophet unto the nations.

The ABC's of Spiritual Identity

PRAYER: *Father, the longest day that I live, I will never understand why You chose to use me in Your Salvation Plan! Filthy, wretched and dirty...I could not even help myself! Surely, I was in no condition to help anyone else! But through Your amazing power, you fashioned me for your cause. Now I am a sanctified vessel, better than I ever was!! Amen!!*

Triumphant

State or condition of having gained the victory over an opponent, adversary or a contender; the declared winner over another in a fight, contest or challenge; victorious; successful.

1 Corinthians 2:14a Now thanks be unto God, which always causeth us to triumph, in Christ...

PRAYER: Jehovah Sabaoth, You are the God of angel armies!! You surround

Your people, protecting us from all of the forces of evil. Therefore, we have no need to fear. You are always here, fighting for us! You will never leave nor forsake us!! You will never abandon us, nor will you ever fail us! We can trust that because You are the Greatest Power, we shall never, ever be defeated!! Amen!!

U

I Am the "Un"

<u>Un -</u> *prefix that when it is attached to another word, changes the meaning of that word to mean the opposite of its original meaning.*

The enemy attacks the believer's spiritual identity. He continually reminds us of our past failures and the labels that we were previously identified by!

The paralyzing effect of fear immobilizes us from moving into the future God has planned for us. Our own fear of failure causes us to not only question our spiritual identity; but, to also disqualify ourselves from reaching the level of "greatness" God says is ours.

Galatians 2:20 _I am crucified with Christ: nevertheless I live; yet not I, but Christ liveth in me: and the life which I now live in the flesh I live by the faith of the Son of God, who loved me, and gave himself for me._

PRAYER: _Thank you Jesus for new life and a new identity!! Through baptism, the old me was buried underneath a watery grave! The new me was resurrected to walk in the newness of life! I am who You say that I am! Now, I can do all things through Christ which strengthens me! Amen!!_

The ABC's of Spiritual Identity

V

Valuable

Having worth; regarded as useful, important, significant, meaningful and vital; greatly appreciated.

Genesis 1:27 *And ye shall be hated of all men for my name's sake: but he that endureth to the end shall be saved. Fear ye not therefore, ye are of more value than many sparrows.*

Luke 12:6b, 7 *[(verse 6b - paraphrased) And not one sparrow is forgotten* before God.] But even the very hairs of your head is numbered. Fear not therefore: ye are of more value than many sparrows.

PRAYER: Kind and compassionate God, I cannot begin to comprehend the depth of Your unconditional love for me!! You demonstrated that I was valuable to you in that while I was yet a sinner, Jesus Christ, your dear Son, died for me! You saw my hidden value, even beyond my faults, failures and imperfections. For this, You deserve my utmost reverence and adoration!! All glory belongs to You!! Amen!!

W

Who God Says I Am

The topic of discussion is "spiritual identity." Is it the "me" that you perceive, or the "me" that God knows, that matters? The answer to this question is clearly obvious! My "real" identity is founded in, "who God says I am!"

Throughout our lifetime, there will be many voices that shall come to influence how we identify ourselves. Therefore, it is important that we know how to distinguish God's voice from other voices that are not his. We cannot afford to be defined, or guided, by other voices.

St. John 10:14, 27 NIV *I am the good shepherd; I know my sheep and my sheep know me. My sheep listen to my voice; I know them, and they follow me.*

PRAYER: Holy God, may we always walk close enough to you to know and to discern you from imposters. May our ears be keenly tuned to hear what you say in spite of all of the chatter, noise and other disguised voices!! May we remember that what you say is all that matters! In Jesus Name...Amen!!

The ABC's of Spiritual Identity

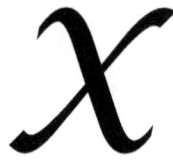

[A] Xerophyte

A plant that loses very little water and can grow in deserts or very dry ground. The spiritual application of a "xerophyte" is this. Christian believers continue to "thrive" in this world that is not designed for us to even "survive" in it!

Isaiah 53:2 And he shall grow up before him as a tender plant, and as a root out of dry ground: he hath no form nor comeliness; and when we shall see him, there is no beauty that we should desire him.

PRAYER: God, You are our Source! You are water in dry places! You make ways out of no way. Lord God, without You we would cease to be!! This world is not our home. As sojourners, nothing about life here on earth is easy, comfortable or convenient for us. So, continue to help us navigate this strange land until the day that You return to take us home with You, to live forever in Your Presence! Amen!!

The ABC's of Spiritual Identity

y

[A] **Yokefellow** *of Jesus Christ*

A person who is joined or united with another in a task; a partner; a co-laborer. This definition points to our Covenant relationship with God in ministry.

<u>Genesis 1:27</u> For we are labourers together with God: ye are God's husbandry[1], ye are God's building[2].

---

[1] Husbandry – the management of our affairs is God's responsibility.
[2] Building – God is the architect; He designs the blueprint; He outlines the floorplan; God oversees the project and assembles the structure.

PRAYER: *God, how I thank You for the privilege to be seated with You in heavenly places in Christ Jesus!! I am humbled that You desire to be in "covenant relationship" with me! Thank You for the many ministry doors and opportunities You have opened unto me! Thank You for entrusting me with revelations hidden in Your Word!! Most of all, God, I thank You for the priceless gift of salvation! I now walk in liberty and I live free from sin because of the divine exchange at Calvary!! Amen!!*

The ABC's of Spiritual Identity

Z

[A] Zionist

<u>Zion</u> - *A fortified place; the hill of Jerusalem on which the city of David was built [3]; The promised land; a citadel [4] that was in the center of Jerusalem, which explains why Zion also means highest point. The "<u>Zionist</u>" is one who considers that the things of God are worth fighting for. No, our fight is not a physical one fought with carnal weapons. But, we engage in*

---

[3] Read 2 Samuel 5 concerning David's daring and strategic capture and takeover of Zion

[4] Citadel – fortress commanding a city; a strongly fortified place; a stronghold; a strong, safe place; a place of refuge

"spiritual warfare," using the weapons of prayer, fasting, the Word and praise to conquer our adversaries!

Matthew 11:12 And from the days of John the Baptist until now the kingdom of heaven suffereth violence, and the violent take it by force.

PRAYER: God, thank you for teaching our hands to war! Thank you for elevating our mindsets to consider that the things of God are a more worthwhile pursuit than fighting to have material things and money! Amen!!

About The Author

Lottie Alexander was born in San Antonio, Texas; but grew up in, and is currently a resident of Houston, Texas. She is the mother of two adult children, the grandmother of eight and the great-grandmother of five.

Lottie has worked in the Administrative Clerical field since May 1977. Lottie's current employment, for the past twenty plus years, is as an Administrative Assistant with Harris County.

Lottie graduated from Evan E. Worthing High School, Houston, Texas. She later attended vocational training and received certification in Data Entry and Word Processing. As a previous "Inspire Women" scholarship recipient, Lottie was privileged to attend the College of Biblical Studies - Houston, Texas, where her fields of study were Bible Study Methods and Biblical Worldview.

Lottie received her Minister's License from the Pentecostal Assemblies of the World organization (PAW Inc.), while attending the Christ Temple Apostolic Church (CTAC) in Houston, Texas. She received Ministers Development certification from The Fountain of Praise (TFOP) Church in Houston, Texas.

Lottie is currently a member of the Greater Grace Houston church family, under the leadership of Apostle E.L. Usher and Pastor Tawanda LaShun Usher. She functions there as an intercessor and an affirmed five-fold ministry teacher.

Lottie's other organizational affiliations include Bread of Life Prison Ministry (Chaplain Carl and Lady Bridgette Farris), Faith Beyond Incarceration Prison Ministry

(Minister Albert Yancey III) and Open Doors Prison Ministry (Minister Sean Oliver). Lottie is also a member of The Women of Valor Global Network, Founder Dr. Allison Wiley.

Lottie is the Founder of two social media ministries - RAHIM (Restoration and Healing Intercession Ministries) and The Waiting Room Encourager Network (WREN) Ministries. In addition to being an author, Lottie is also a psalmist, instrumentalist, and songwriter.

"My desire to minister to other hurting women is fueled by my own "real-life" experiences with emotional trauma. Thankfully, because of the grace of God, I can testify today that I am healed, whole and complete in Him!"

Lottie believes her assignment is to share God's message of salvation and hope with those who are seeking after Him. She shares that her passion is *helping others discover their own God-given purpose. Her testimony is that, "It was that discovery that helped me to make sense of my life."*

www.ingramcontent.com/pod-product-compliance
Lightning Source LLC
Chambersburg PA
CBHW071230160426
43196CB00012B/2465